D1124369

	DATE DUE	

TREATIES AND RESOLUTIONS

By Sheila Rivera

VISIT US AT
WWW.ABDOPUB.COM

Published by ABDO & Daughters, an imprint of ABDO Publishing Company, 4940 Viking Drive, Suite 622, Edina, Minnesota 55435.

Printed in the United States.

Edited by: Cory Gunderson
Contributing Editors: Paul Joseph, Chris Schafer
Graphic Design: Arturo Leyva, David Bullen
Cover Design: Castaneda Dunham, Inc.
Photos: Corbis, Fotosearch

Library of Congress Cataloging-in-Publication Data

Rivera, Sheila, 1970-
   Treaties and resolutions / Sheila Rivera.
    p. cm. -- (World in conflict--the Middle East)
   Includes index.
   Summary: Discusses efforts to find a solution to the conflict between Israelis and Palestinians, focusing on four specific peace negotiations in the past thirty-five years.
   ISBN 1-59197-420-8
    1. Arab-Israeli conflict--1993---Peace--Juvenile literature. [1. Arab-Israeli conflict--1993---Peace.] I. Title. II. World in conflict (Edina, Minn.). Middle East.

   DS119.76.R586 2003
   956.04--dc21

                  2003043743

TABLE OF CONTENTS

Palestinian women protesting Israeli aggression

OVERVIEW OF PEACE NEGOTIATIONS

The history of Israel is one filled with fighting. Israel and Palestine are two territories located in the Middle East. These two nations have been fighting for control of the same land. They have disputed boundary lines for more than 50 years. Israel has also fought against Egypt, Syria, Lebanon, and Jordan. These countries have supported Palestine because, like Palestine, they are Muslim nations. Israel is a Jewish nation.

War and violence occur frequently in the small country of Israel. There have also been numerous attempts to resolve the conflicts. Most Middle Eastern people want peace in their region. Most also want it only on their own terms.

Many peace talks and agreements have been negotiated since Israel's War of Independence in 1948. Several negotiations stand apart. One important resolution in Israeli-Arab history is United Nations Resolution 242. It came after the Six Day War in 1967. A second important negotiation was the Camp David Accord and the peace treaty that followed it in 1979. A third important peace agreement was reached in 1993. Part of that agreement was the Oslo Declaration of Principles. A fourth important negotiation was the 1998 Wye River Memorandum.

You might wonder why there have been so many peace talks. Wouldn't one peace agreement be enough to fix the problems between Israel and its neighbors? Unfortunately, the situation is not that simple. Not all of the peace agreements have had the same goals. Not all have involved the same people either. That's why peace has yet to be established in the Middle East.

Crowd cheering in Cairo, Egypt, prior to the signing of the Camp David Accord

UNITED NATIONS RESOLUTION 242

Tension due to the Israeli-Palestinian land dispute had been building in the Middle East for years. In 1964, Arab leaders created the Palestine Liberation Organization (PLO). The organization's goal was to fight Israel and return Israeli land to Arab power.

At the same time, tension was also high between the United States and the Soviet Union. The U.S. and the Soviet Union were not directly involved in the Israeli-Palestinian conflict. The U.S. did, though, give military and political support to Israel. And the Soviets supplied Palestine with military weapons. This outside influence fueled the fire between Israel and Palestine.

Israel's Arab neighbors, meanwhile, were working against Israel. During the 1960s, Israel developed a National Water

Carrier Plan. Under this plan, Israel took water from the Sea of Galilee, between Israel and Syria. It then pumped the water into the lower regions of Israel. Syria, Jordan, and Lebanon wanted to prevent Israel from using this water. These countries changed the course of the Jordan River to reduce Israel's water supply. Israel responded by firing on the Syrian workers. This was only the beginning of what would soon become an all-out war between Israel and its Arab neighbors.

On Israel's southwest border, Egypt was also making a plan. In May of 1967, Egypt closed the Strait of Tiran between Egypt and Israel. Egypt also sent UN peacekeepers out of Sinai. Both of these actions were considered acts of war. In addition, Egypt's President Nasser made statements against Israel and signed a defense pact with Jordan.

With tension growing, several Arab nations began talking about invading Israel. Egypt attempted to unite the Arab nations in 1967 and discussed an invasion. Before the Arab nations could act, though, Israel attacked its enemies. The Israeli army wiped out the entire air power of Egypt, Syria, Iraq, and Jordan. Israel's military was powerful. Within six days, Israel had taken the Sinai Peninsula and the Gaza Strip from Egypt. It took the

United Nations Resolution 242

SYRIA

HAIFA

MEDITERRANEAN SEA

JORDAN RIVER

TEL
AVIV

JERUSALEM

DEAD
SEA

BETHLEHEM

EGYPT

ISRAEL

JORDAN

BEERSHEBA

SINAI
PENINSULA

Israeli territorial boundaries established by the UN in 1948

SYRIA

HAIFA

Golan
Heights

West
Bank

MEDITERRANEAN SEA

JORDAN RIVER

TEL
AVIV

JERUSALEM

BETHLEHEM

DEAD
SEA

Gaza
Strip

ISRAEL

JORDAN

EGYPT

BEERSHEBA

SINAI
PENINSULA

After the Six Day War in 1967, Israel controlled the Gaza Strip, the Sinai Peninsula, the West Bank, and the Golan Heights.

Golan Heights from Syria and the West Bank and East Jerusalem from Jordan. Israel's well organized and well armed military pushed the Arab forces back one by one. Eventually, each one of them gave up. On June 11, 1967, Israel stopped fighting. The UN stepped in to try to bring peace to the Middle East. It proposed a peace plan known as UN Resolution 242.

The Proposal

After the Six Day War ended, the UN General Assembly met. Members of the assembly discussed the problem surrounding the nation of Israel. Their goal was to bring a peaceful solution to the problem. The heart of the problem was the Arab demand that Israel leave the territories it conquered. There were also disputes regarding the location of the borders. There were disagreements, too, regarding from which locations the Israelis were to withdraw. The General Assembly referred the issue to its Security Council.

The UN drew up a peace plan called UN Resolution 242. Its requirements were:

- Israel had to withdraw its armed forces from the territories it conquered in the Six Day War.

- Every nation was ordered to respect the others' boundaries.

- Each nation was to let other nations self-rule without being threatened.

- The UN created demilitarized zones. No military could be present in these zones. They were established so that each country felt safe from other countries.

- The Middle East nations were called to recognize and respect each other. This included recognizing and respecting Israel's independence.

- International waterways were to be open to every nation.

- The problem of the Palestinian refugees was to be resolved.

- The UN Secretary General would assign a special representative to keep in touch with each nation. This representative was to help the countries come to a peace agreement.

- The Secretary General should report back to the UN. His report includes the status of the special representative's efforts.

    The British Ambassador presented the resolution's final draft to the UN on November 22, 1967. It was accepted that same day.

The United Nations Security Council meets to discuss the conflict in the MIddle East.

The Outcome

After the resolution was signed, Israel agreed to return all conquered territories except Jerusalem. The Arab nations still refused to accept Israel as an independent nation. The objectives of the resolution were not met. Israel kept its military in the West Bank and the Gaza Strip. These territories were considered occupied territories. Israel also maintained control over East Jerusalem and considered it a part of its land.

The Palestinian refugee problem was not solved either. Many Palestinians had fled from their homes during the Israeli War of Independence in 1948. These refugees continued to live in camps in Israeli-occupied Palestine and in neighboring Arab countries.

The Palestinian refugees began to feel like they didn't belong to the greater Arab nation. They believed that they would need to rely on themselves to solve the conflict. They felt stronger ties to one another because of the suffering they endured. The Palestinians formed several radical groups to fight for their rights.

Radical groups such as Al Fatah continued to attack Israel despite UN Resolution 242. Egypt and Syria would no longer allow Palestinian groups to attack Israel from their nations. Still, the Palestinian radicals were not discouraged. They moved their forces to Lebanon and Jordan and continued to attack from there. A second cease-fire was signed in 1970. Both Israel and Palestine accepted UN Resolution 242 under pressure from the U.S.

A Jordanian girl holds a Koran during a rally in the Palestinian refugee camp of Bagaa.

CAMP DAVID ACCORD

In September 1970, Egyptian President Nasser died. Anwar Sadat became Egypt's new president. Sadat had been Nasser's vice president. His goals for Egypt were to establish peace and prosperity.

Former President Nasser had closed the Suez Canal between Sinai and greater Egypt. Sadat offered to open the canal if Israel would give portions of Sinai back to Egypt. Israel refused Egypt's offer. Egypt began to restore its relationship with the U.S. It also worked to improve relations with other Arab nations.

In 1977, Israel elected Menachem Begin its new prime minister. Begin offered to return Sinai to Egyptian power if Egypt would make peace with Israel.

During the mid 1970s, the Palestine Liberation Organization (PLO) was also undergoing some changes. The PLO

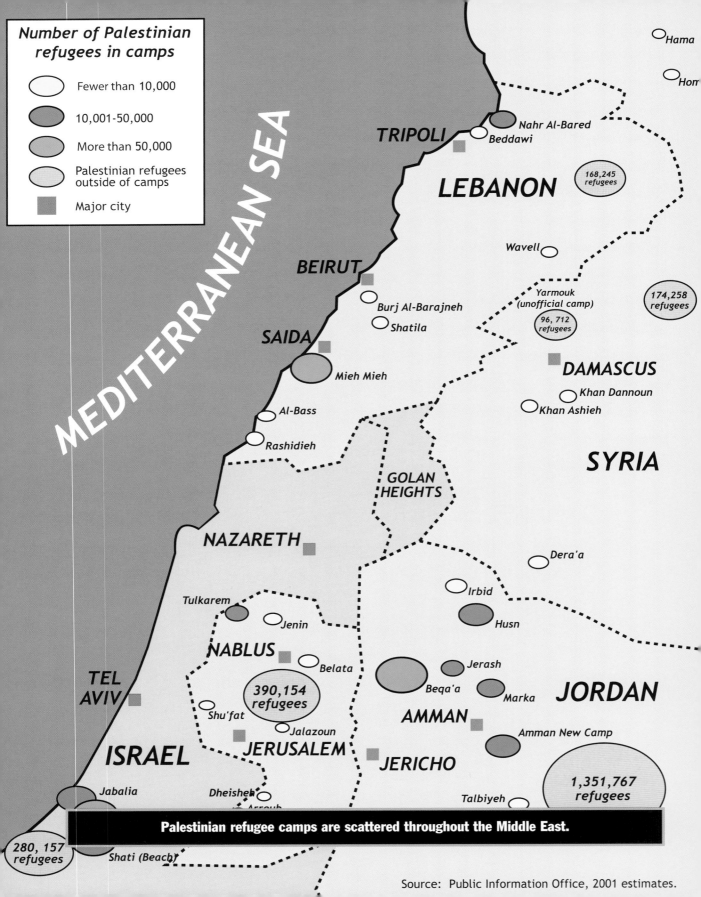

Number of Palestinian refugees in camps

- Fewer than 10,000
- 10,001–50,000
- More than 50,000
- Palestinian refugees outside of camps
- Major city

MEDITERRANEAN SEA

TRIPOLI

Nahr Al-Bared
Beddawi

LEBANON

168,245 refugees

Wavell

BEIRUT

Burj Al-Barajneh
Shatila

Yarmouk (unofficial camp)

174,258 refugees

96,712 refugees

SAIDA

DAMASCUS

Mieh Mieh

Khan Dannoun

Khan Ashieh

Al-Bass

SYRIA

Rashidieh

GOLAN HEIGHTS

NAZARETH

Dera'a

Irbid

Tulkarem

Jenin

Husn

NABLUS

Jerash

Belata

TEL AVIV

390,154 refugees

Beqa'a

Marka

JORDAN

Shu'fat

AMMAN

Jalazoun

ISRAEL

JERUSALEM

JERICHO

Amman New Camp

Jabalia

Dheisheh

Talbiyeh

1,351,767 refugees

Arroub

280,157 refugees

Shati (Beach)

Palestinian refugee camps are scattered throughout the Middle East.

Hama

Hom

Source: Public Information Office, 2001 estimates.

had previously done whatever it took to regain Palestine for the Palestinian people. This had included terrorism and the use of military force. During the mid 1970s, the PLO began to use more diplomatic means to achieve its goal. In 1974, the PLO began to change its focus away from terrorism. Its new focus led to PLO recognition by the UN for the first time. The possibility for peace in the Middle East looked promising.

In November 1977, Egyptian President Sadat made a bold step. He offered to visit Israel and talk to its legislature, the Knesset. Relations between Israel and Egypt had been bad for so long. Both leaders, though, were willing to negotiate peace. Israeli President Begin extended an invitation for the visit.

Sadat spoke to the Knesset on November 19, 1977. He explained his view of the Middle East conflict. The core issue, as he saw it, was the need for a Palestinian homeland. He asked for the return of Egyptian territory taken by Israel in the 1967 war. Sadat also acknowledged the nation of Israel. Sadat's visit was the start of peace negotiations that led to the Camp David Peace Accord.

Camp David Peace Talks

Peace talks between Israel and Egypt slowed in 1978. The two nations needed help to come to a formal peace agreement.

Camp David Accord

The U.S. stepped in to help. U.S. President Jimmy Carter invited President Sadat and Prime Minister Begin to the U.S. The three leaders met at the presidential retreat in Camp David, Maryland, in September 1978. By the tenth day of the talks, Begin and Sadat weren't speaking to one another. Sadat declared that the talks were over and he was leaving. President Carter persuaded him to stay. Carter was eventually able to help the two parties draft a peace plan. The U.S. supported the peace plan by promising aid to both countries.

The Proposal

Sadat and Begin agreed on a peace plan called the Camp David Accord. The main points of the accord were:

- The Israeli armed forces would withdraw from Sinai.
- Egypt and Israel would recognize each other as independent nations. They would act peacefully toward one another.
- Israel would be able to use the Suez Canal.
- There would eventually be talks to decide on Palestinian rule in the West Bank and Gaza.
- Conflicts between the two parties would be resolved in a peaceful manner. If the two governments could not settle a dispute, a third party, called a mediator, would help.

Jimmy Carter smiles as Menachem Begin and Anwar Sadat embrace after signing the Camp David Accord.

The Outcome

Sadat and Begin received Nobel Peace Prizes for their efforts in this peace plan. Parts of the plan were successful. After the peace agreement, Israel began withdrawing from Sinai. Israel gave full control of Sinai back to Egypt in 1982. Egypt also opened the waters of the Suez Canal to Israel as promised. The two countries did business with each other. They even built embassies in one another's country.

The Camp David Accord was not a complete success, however. A plan for creating Palestinian rule in the West Bank and Gaza never happened. Israelis continued to settle in Palestinian areas. Arab nations were angry at Egypt for recognizing Israel. They called President Sadat a traitor and kicked Egypt out of the Arab League. Many Arab nations also stopped doing business with Egypt. In 1981, Islamic extremists killed Sadat. The extremists did not approve of his peace negotiations with Israel.

MEDITERRANEAN SEA

TEL AVIV

WEST BANK

JERUSALEM

GAZA CITY

GAZA STRIP

PORT SAID

CAIRO

ISRAEL

SUEZ CANAL

EGYPT

SINAI PENINSULA

J
O
R
D
A
N

SUEZ

GULF OF SUEZ

AQABA

The West Bank, the Gaza Strip, and the Sinai Peninsula have been sources of conflict for many years.

RED SEA

DAHAB

1993 PEACE AGREEMENT/OSLO DECLARATION OF PRINCIPLES

The PLO continued its violent tactics against Israel into the 1970s. In the early 1980s, the Israeli military, under Ariel Sharon, took severe measures against the PLO. Israel attacked the PLO in Lebanon. The PLO was forced to move its base out of Lebanon and into Tunis. Tunis is the capital of Tunisia on the north African coast. The Israelis attacked Palestinian civilians in refugee camps. This enraged the Palestinians. The result was the formation of an extremist anti-Israel terror group. This terror group is called Hamas.

In other countries in the region, problems were mounting as well. In the early 1990s, Iraq invaded Kuwait. The U.S. declared war on Iraq in defense of Kuwait. This conflict was called the Gulf War. The Gulf War increased tension in the Middle East. At the war's end, the need for peace in the Middle East became an international priority. The focus turned back to Israel and Palestine.

Making Peace Plans

In late 1991, Lebanon, Syria, Israel, and a joint Jordanian-Palestinian delegation began peace talks. The U.S. and Russia sponsored the peace talks in Madrid, Spain. They also sponsored talks in the U.S. the following year. Israel, Palestine, Jordan, Lebanon, and Syria were all urged to attend. The Madrid Peace Conference was unsuccessful. Israel's government under Yitzhak Shamir was reluctant to make any agreements. Little progress was made. Israel elected Prime Minister Yitzhak Rabin to office in 1992. Rabin was committed to peace negotiations and took steps toward an agreement. Israeli and Palestinian leaders decided to take matters into their own hands.

Declaration of Principles

While the Madrid Peace Conference was stalling, Israeli and Palestinian representatives met secretly in Oslo, Norway. The Norwegian foreign minister hosted peace talks between the two groups.

During the Oslo peace talks, Israel was willing to deal directly with the PLO. The Palestinians were permitted to speak for themselves in matters that directly affected them. The two nations drew up a plan for peace. They called the plan the Declaration of Principles on Interim Self-Government Arrangement. The simpler name was the Declaration of Principles.

Will peace ever prevail? Palestinians burn an Israeli flag.

The Declaration of Principles described a plan for an interim, or temporary, Palestinian self-government authority. Israeli Prime Minister Yitzhak Rabin and Palestinian leader Yasser Arafat signed the final peace agreement in Washington, D.C. U.S. President Bill Clinton hosted the September 13, 1993, signing of the peace agreement.

The Proposal

The major points of the plan were:

- Both Israel and Palestine would recognize and respect one another's right to exist. This meant that the PLO would have to accept Israel as a nation. It had to stop its terrorist activities toward Israel.
- Israel would withdraw from areas of the West Bank and Gaza Strip.
- The Palestinians would elect an interim Palestinian government.
- There would be a gradual change to Palestinian control in the West Bank and the Gaza Strip.
- Israel and Palestine would commit themselves to the creation of a permanent settlement within five years.
- Conflicts between the two nations would be settled by a joint committee.
- Within three years, a plan would be made regarding refugees, settlements, borders, and Jerusalem.

The Outcome

In 1993, the Israeli Knesset reversed the law that had been passed in 1986. This law had made it illegal for Israelis to have contact with the PLO. This reversal made it easier for Israel and Palestine to deal with one another.

By 1994, it looked like the peace plan was progressing. The Palestinian police force took over administration of the Gaza Strip and Jericho. The Palestinians elected their new government called the Palestinian National Authority. The Palestinian National Authority took control of education, social welfare, and economics in much of the West Bank. An increasing number of Palestinians returned to work in the West Bank. The plan appeared successful because it gave Palestinians some control over their lands. Unfortunately, it left too many issues unresolved.

Among the issues were the Israeli settlements, the status of Jerusalem, official Palestinian and Israeli borders, and the refugee problem. Israel maintained settlements in the Palestinian areas and continued to settle there. This made the separation of the two independent nations difficult. It also frustrated Palestinians.

A Palestinian woman looks out from a refugee camp.

Concrete borders were not established. This caused conflict over disputed areas. One of the most disputed areas was the city of Jerusalem. Israel and Palestine have fought over Jerusalem because of its religious importance to both Jews and Muslims.

The last and probably biggest issue that remained unsolved was a plan for Palestinian refugees. Thousands of refugees were living in refugee camps in the occupied territories and neighboring countries. No plan was made to bring them back into Palestine. Many refugees remained in the camps.

The peace plan didn't offer any solutions to these important issues. This meant that the peace plan was not completely successful.

WYE RIVER MEMORANDUM

During the years following the 1993 peace agreement, violence continued in Israel. Some Palestinians disagreed with the 1993 peace agreement. They felt that Arafat should not have agreed to allow Israel to control any Arab land. Some Islamic extremist groups felt that there was only one answer to the Israeli-Palestinian conflict. The extremists wanted Israel to return all of its land to Palestinian control. The Islamic extremist group Hamas carried out suicide bombings throughout Israel. Israel tried to maintain control over Palestinians. It did so by frequently closing off Palestinian-governed areas from Israel and the other occupied territories. The fighting continued.

The Proposal

In 1995, Israeli Prime Minister Yitzhak Rabin was killed at a peace rally by Jewish fundamentalist Yigal Amir. Shimon Peres was elected prime minister in his place. Peres pledged to carry out the promises of Rabin. This included his involvement in the peace plan with Palestine and other Arab nations.

Again, the U.S. wanted to help the Middle East peace process. The Israeli-Palestinian Interim Agreement on the West Bank and Gaza Strip was signed in Washington, D.C. This 1995 agreement was supposed to help Israel and Palestine carry out the 1993 agreement.

On December 27, 1995, peace talks began in the U.S. Officials from Israel and Syria talked over the course of a month. They met near the Wye River in the state of Maryland.

The talks focused on issues including roadways, telecommunications, and embassies. They also talked about ending Arab boycotts on Israeli products. Arab nations had refused to buy Israeli goods. They believed that this practice would weaken the Israeli economy and help the Palestinians. By ending the ban it would increase the chances for peaceful relations.

The talks also addressed security and the Golan Heights. Prime Minister Peres felt that the progress was going too slow. The talks ended for a time after Hamas attacked a group of Israelis in Jerusalem.

Palestinian boys chant anti-Israel slogans during a rally against the Wye River Memorandum.

In 1996, Israel held elections. Prime Minister Peres lost to Benjamin Netanyahu. Violence between Israelis and Palestinians continued to erupt. In 1998, U.S. President Bill Clinton hosted another summit meeting at Wye River. Netanyahu and Yasser Arafat signed the Wye River Memorandum on October 23, 1998, in Washington, D.C. King Hussein of Jordan also attended the signing ceremony. The memorandum explained how Israel and Palestine could carry out the 1995 Interim Agreement.

The main points of the Wye River Memorandum were to:
- End Palestinian terrorism and violence.
- Set up guidelines for Israel to pull its forces out of more territory.
- Transfer a larger portion of the West Bank to Palestinian control.
- Outline a security plan for Israel.
- Make a plan for talks regarding the creation of a formal Palestinian state.
- Open safe travel routes between Gaza and the West Bank.

The Outcome

In December 1998, Palestinian and Israeli leaders continued to meet. The meetings were a promising part of the peace process. Still, the reality was that neither side had kept the promises made at the peace conference. The situation between the two groups was getting worse.

By mid December, Israel refused to pull back its troops as it had pledged. Israeli leaders felt that Palestine was not holding up its end of the peace agreements. Israelis and Palestinians continued to fight.

Both Israeli and Palestinian leaders continued to talk about peace. It was clear, though, that they lacked confidence in their ability to carry out the plan. In 1998, Prime Minister Netanyahu said, "What we must ensure is a peace which will endure for decades and not for the next newscast."

Israeli soldiers arrest a Palestinian youth during anti-settlement protests in the West Bank.

RECENT PEACE TALKS

There have been many attempts in recent years to achieve peace between Palestine and Israel. In July of 1999, Palestinian President Yasser Arafat said, "It is time to put an end to the cycle of violence and confrontation." Israel's Prime Minister at that time, Ehud Barak, also wanted to work toward peace.

The two leaders met in Gaza to examine what progress had been made under the Wye River Memorandum. Both stated that they wanted to do what they had agreed upon. Still, they had different ideas on a few issues. Arafat stated, "Settlement activities are illegal and destructive to the peace process." He asked the Israelis to stop settling in Palestinian territories. Israel had agreed to give up larger portions of the West Bank. Jewish people, though, continued to settle there. The Palestinians did not think this was fair, but they agreed to continue peace talks.

In 2000, violence raged between the Israelis and the Palestinians. The two leaders continued to talk of peace. Still, they could not agree on the issue of borders or the status of Jerusalem. Palestinians wanted control of all of East Jerusalem, but Israel would not agree to it. The two nations could not agree on Palestinian borders either. Without agreeing on these two issues, they could not make progress toward peace. Palestinians did not want the issue of Jerusalem to stop all progress.

U.S. President Bill Clinton tried again to help Israel and Palestine find a peaceful solution. He arranged another peace meeting at Camp David. After 15 days of talking, Israel and Palestine could not agree on a plan. The talks ended without an agreement. Both leaders realized that they probably wouldn't make an agreement that year.

Through 2001, the Palestinian group Islamic Jihad carried out suicide bombings in Israeli cities. In return, Israeli forces killed a leader of the Popular Front for the Liberation of Palestine. Palestinian forces followed up by killing the Israeli tourism minister.

In 2002, Israel took severe measures against Palestinians. In March, Arafat was imprisoned in his own compound. Israeli troops attacked people in a Palestinian refugee camp and

"Free Palestine" poster with Bill Clinton and Yasser Arafat

destroyed their homes. Dozens of people were killed. The UN Security Council stepped in. It passed Resolution 1397. The formal statement demanded that both sides stop the violence. It required that a Palestinian state be created.

In May 2002, Arafat signed the Palestine Basic Law. It outlined basic rights for the Palestinian people, but they are not clear. It declared Jerusalem the capital of Palestine. The Palestinian National Authority, though, has no official control over that area.

Most people in Israel and Palestine want peace between their nations. They have different ideas, though, about the land that they are fighting for. Both sides want certain areas of land. Neither side is willing to give up what they feel they have a right to. A peaceful solution seems as far off as it ever has.

FAST FACTS

- The city of Jerusalem is one of the most significant and disputed areas in the Middle East. It is considered a holy city by Muslims, Jews, and Christians.
- The Palestine Liberation Organization (PLO) was created in 1964. The group's goal was to fight Israel and return Israeli land to Arab power.
- Over decades, numerous attempts have been made by the United Nations to bring Israel and Palestine to a peaceful resolution. No lasting peace has been reached.
- Most of the United Nations' Middle East peace negotiations have involved Israel.
- The U.S has been Israel's most powerful supporter in its conflicts.
- For their efforts in working towards peace, Nobel Peace Prizes were awarded to Middle East leaders Yasser Arafat, Shimon Peres, Yitzhak Rabin, Anwar Sadat, and Menachem Begin.
- In 1981, Islamic extremists killed Anwar Sadat.
- Many Islamic extremists are opposed to sharing any Arab land with Israel.
- Many peace negotiations have failed because of terrorist actions.
- In 2002, former U.S. President Jimmy Carter received a Nobel Peace Prize for his involvement in the Camp David Accords as well as for other peace-making initiatives.

TIMELINE

1948	Israel establishes itself as a homeland for the Jewish people. The Arab world resents the Jewish control of what they see as Muslim land.
1964	Arab leaders create the Palestine Liberation Organization (PLO).
1967	Egypt closes the Strait of Tiran between Egypt and Israel.
1970	Israel and Palestine accept UN Resolution 242 under pressure from the U.S.
1974	The PLO is first recognized by the UN as the voice for the Palestinian people.
1977	Israel elects Menachem Begin as its Prime Minister. Egyptian President Anwar Sadat talks to Israel's legislature, the Knesset, on November 19.
1978	U.S. President Jimmy Carter hosts Sadat and Begin at Camp David to negotiate a peace settlement.

1991   The U.S and Russia sponsor peace talks for Israel, Palestine, Jordan, Lebanon, and Syria.

1992   Israel elects Prime Minister Yitzhak Rabin to office.

1993   U.S. President Bill Clinton hosts the signing of an Israeli-Palestinian agreement.

1995   The Israeli-Palestinian Interim Agreement is signed in Washington, D.C.

1996   Israeli Prime Minister Peres loses the election to Benjamin Netanyahu.

1998   Netanyahu and Arafat sign the Wye River Memorandum on October 23, in Washington, D.C.

2002   Israeli soldiers temporarily imprison Arafat in his own compound. Arafat signs the Palestine Basic Law, which outlines the basic rights of the Palestinian people.

GLOSSARY

accord:
To make an agreement; to bring peace.

Al Fatah:
A radical Palestinian organization.

Arab League:
An association of Arab states set up in 1945 to promote cooperation among its member states.

Arafat, Yasser:
Leader of the Palestine Liberation Organization. In 1996, was elected the first president of the Palestinian National Authority, the newly formed Palestinian self-rule government.

Barak, Ehud:
Politician who was elected Israel's prime minister in 1999.

Begin, Menachem:
Russian-born politician who served as Israel's prime minister from 1977 until 1983.

boycott:
To refrain from dealing with, using, or buying. Used as an expression of protest.

cease-fire:
An order to stop fighting.

compound:
A building or area.

declaration:
A formal announcement that can be either written or oral.

demilitarized zone:
An area which military forces, operations, and installations are prohibited.

Egyptian:
Someone who was born in or lives in the country of Egypt.

Hamas:
A radical Palestinian Muslim group.

interim:
A period of time between one event, process, or period and another.
Islamic extremists:
Muslims who resort to violence in order to defend their religious beliefs.
Israel:
A country in the Middle East that was established in 1948. Considered to be the Jewish homeland.
Israeli-Palestinian conflict:
The decades-long fight between the Jewish Israelis and the Arab Muslims of Palestine over land.
Jerusalem:
The capital of Israel. Also the capital of Palestine under the Palestine Basic Law, signed by Yasser Arafat in 2002. Of religious and historical importance to Jews, Muslims, and Christians.
Jordanian-Palestinian delegation:
A group of people who represented the needs of Jordan's and Palestine's citizens.
Knesset:
Israel's legislature.
mediator:
A person who settles disputes between two parties.
memorandum:
A written document designed for diplomatic communication.
Nasser, Gamal Abdel:
Army officer and politician who served as Egypt's prime minister from 1954 until 1956.
Netanyahu, Benjamin:
Israeli prime minister from 1996 to 1999.
occupied territory:
Territory occupied by Israel.
Palestine:
A historical region in the Middle East that disputes its boundaries with Israel.
Palestine Liberation Organization (PLO):
Coordinating council for Palestinian organizations, founded in 1964. Yasser Arafat has been chairman of the PLO since 1968.
Palestinian National Authority:
Palestine's self-rule government.

Palestinian National Council:
A group of people that decided to create a Palestinian state in the West Bank and the Gaza Strip.

Popular Front for the Liberation of Palestine:
A Palestinian terrorist group.

Rabin, Yitzak:
Served as Israeli prime minister from 1974 to 1977 and from 1992 to 1995.

refugee:
A person who seeks shelter from danger or hardships in times of war or persecution.

resolution:
A course of action.

Sadat, Anwar:
Egypt's prime minister from 1970 to 1981.

Shamir, Yitzhak:
Polish-born leader who was Israel's prime minister from 1983 to 1984 and 1986 to 1990 and 1990 to 1992.

Sinai:
A desert on the Sinai Peninsula in northeastern Egypt.

suicide bomber:
A person who sacrifices their life for political reasons in order to kill others.

summit:
A conference or meeting with high level leaders, usually called to form a program of action.

Syria:
A country in the Middle East. Ancient Syria also included Lebanon, most of present-day Israel and Jordan, and part of Iraq and Saudi Arabia.

telecommunications:
Electronic systems used in transmitting information. Examples are the telegraph, cable, telephone, television, and radio.

United Nations (UN):
An international organization started in 1945 to promote peace, security, and economic development across the world.

WEB SITES
WWW.ABDOPUB.COM

Would you like to learn more about Treaties and Resolutions? Please visit www.abdopub.com to find up-to-date Web site links about Treaties and Resolutions and the World in Conflict. These links are routinely monitored and updated to provide the most current information available.

Israeli man praying in front of the Wailing Wall in Jerusalem

INDEX